PICTURE A
SLAP SHOT ★★★

A Hockey Drawing Book

by Anthony Wacholtz   illustrated by Michael Ray

CAPSTONE PRESS
a capstone imprint

TABLE OF CONTENTS

LET'S HIT THE ICE (AND DRAW!)

It's time to lace up your skates, grab your helmet, and start drawing! Let Sports Illustrated Kids be your guide as you draw yourself into the action on the hockey rink. Are you ready to shuffle the perfect pass? Or make an astounding glove save? But what's more exciting than blasting a slap shot for the winning goal? If you can't decide, draw them all!

Follow the simple step-by-step drawings in this book, and you'll be on your way to hockey stardom. Before you know it, you'll be part of the game. Let's get started!

BEFORE YOU HEAD OUT ON THE ICE, GRAB SOME SUPPLIES:

1. First you'll need drawing paper. Any type of blank, unlined paper will do.

2. Pencils are the easiest to use for your drawing projects. Make sure you have plenty of them.

3. It's easier to make clean lines with sharpened pencils. Keep a pencil sharpener close by.

4. As you practice drawing, you'll need a good eraser. Pencil erasers wear out very quickly. Get a rubber or kneaded eraser.

5. When your drawing is finished, you can trace over it with a black ink pen or a thin felt-tip marker. The dark lines will make your drawing jump off the page.

6. If you decide to color your drawings, colored pencils and markers usually work best. You can also use colored pencils to shade your drawings and make them more lifelike.

STARTING THE SHOT

You bring your stick back as you keep your eyes on the puck and square up toward the goal. Excellent form for a powerful shot!

1

FOLLOW THROUGH

You extend your arms forward through the shot, and the puck blasts toward the goal. The goalie will need a good glove—and some luck—to stop it!

1

CLOSE SHOT

You squeezed past the defenders and received the puck near the goal. Do you have what it takes to sneak a shot past the goalie?

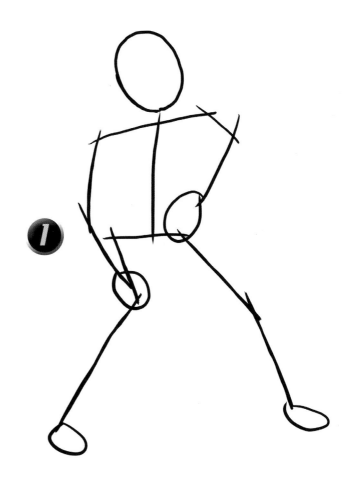

ONE ON ONE

You speed across the open ice with the puck. The only player left to beat is the goalie. You deke to the left, leaving the goalie flailing on the ice. Goal!

MAKE YOUR MOVE

An opponent blocks the way in front of you. Another opponent skates up behind you. Shifting your weight, you veer right while keeping the puck close.

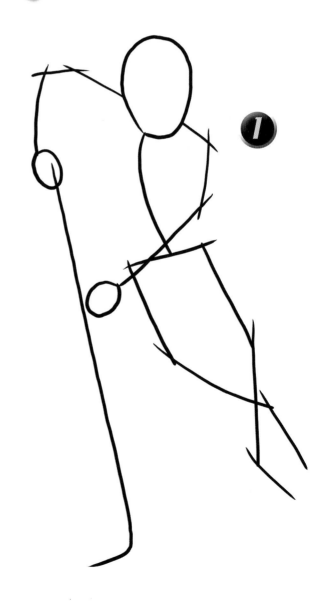

1

READY FOR ANYTHING

Close to the boards, you cradle the puck with your stick. You can pass it off, take a long shot, or cut back for the outside angle. What will you do?

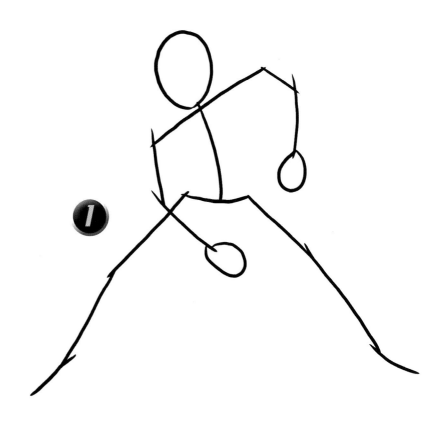

1

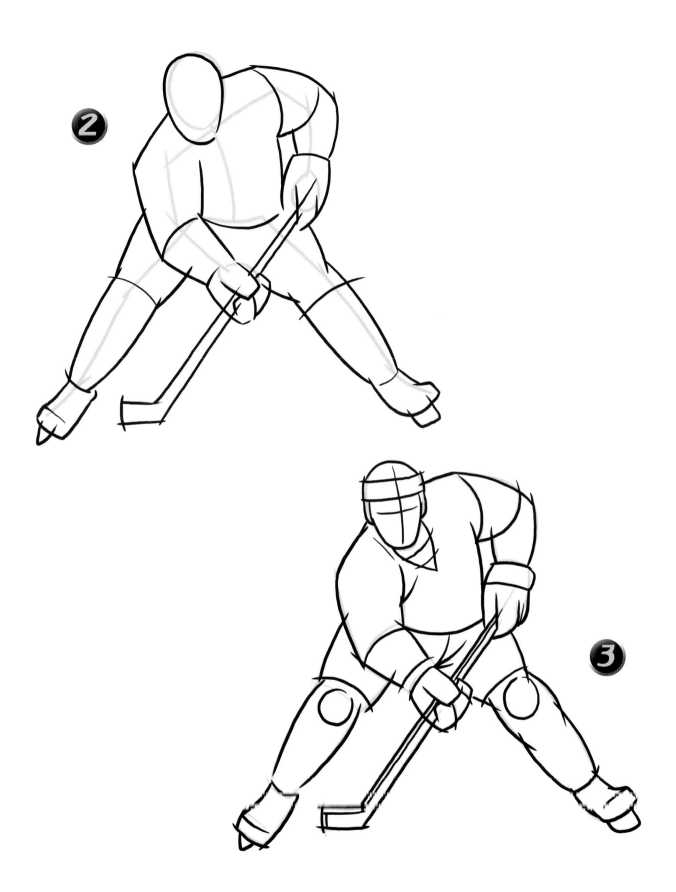

IN THE BOARDS

An opposing player is skating down the ice with the puck. Not so fast! You break toward him and check him into the boards.

1

DEEP IN THE ZONE

You've got the puck near the opponent's goal. All eyes are on you! You bend your knees, lower your stick, and prepare to kick out the puck to a teammate.

1

RACE FOR THE PUCK

The puck slides by everyone and ends up at the edge of the rink. You start skating furiously toward the puck, but two opposing players are right beside you. Who's going to get to it first?

1

FACE OFF

You're hunched over, stick down, eyes focused on the ice. You'll be ready to move as soon as the referee drops the puck. Game on!

1

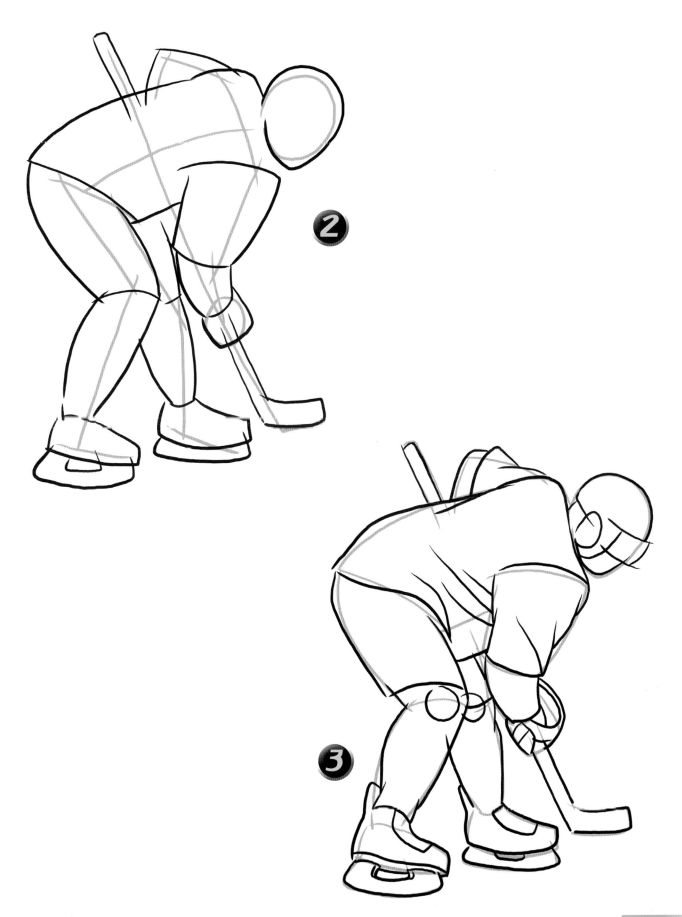

PROTECT THE NET

Here comes the shot! You're all that stands between the puck and the net. You'll do whatever it takes to stop the other team from scoring.

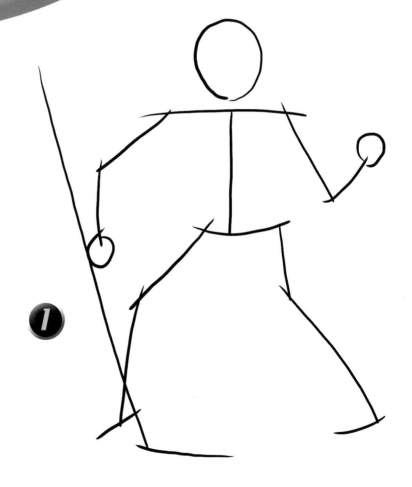

1

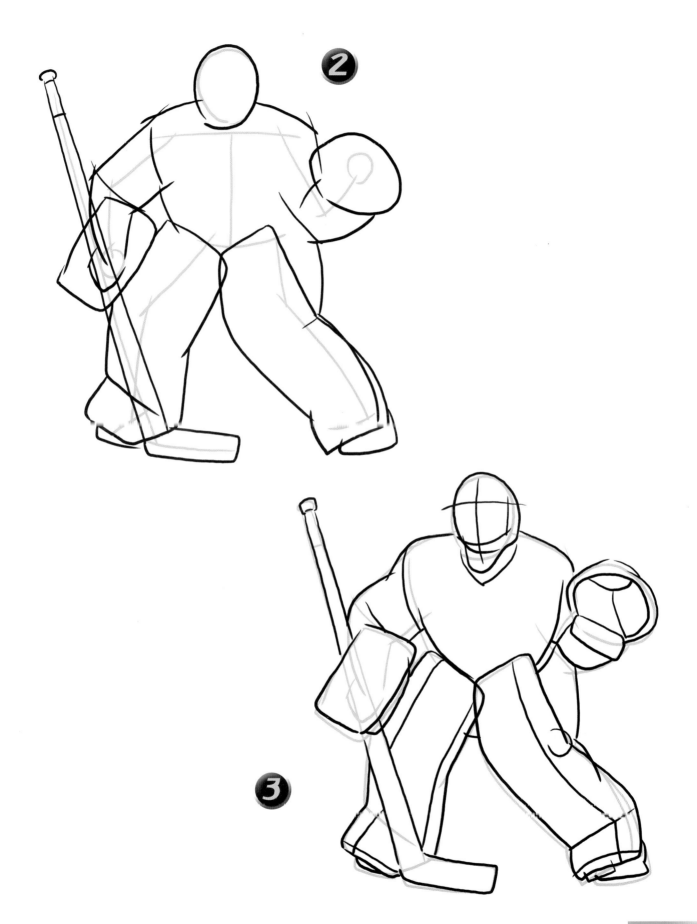

GLOVE SAVE

The puck hurtles toward the net after a powerful slap shot. With lightning-fast reflexes, you reach out with your glove and snag the puck out of the air. What a save!

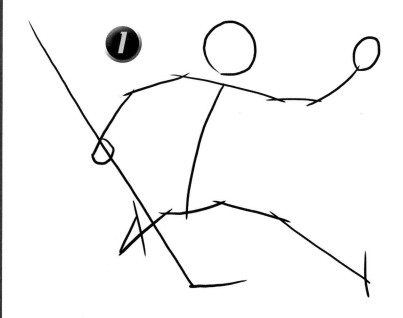

1

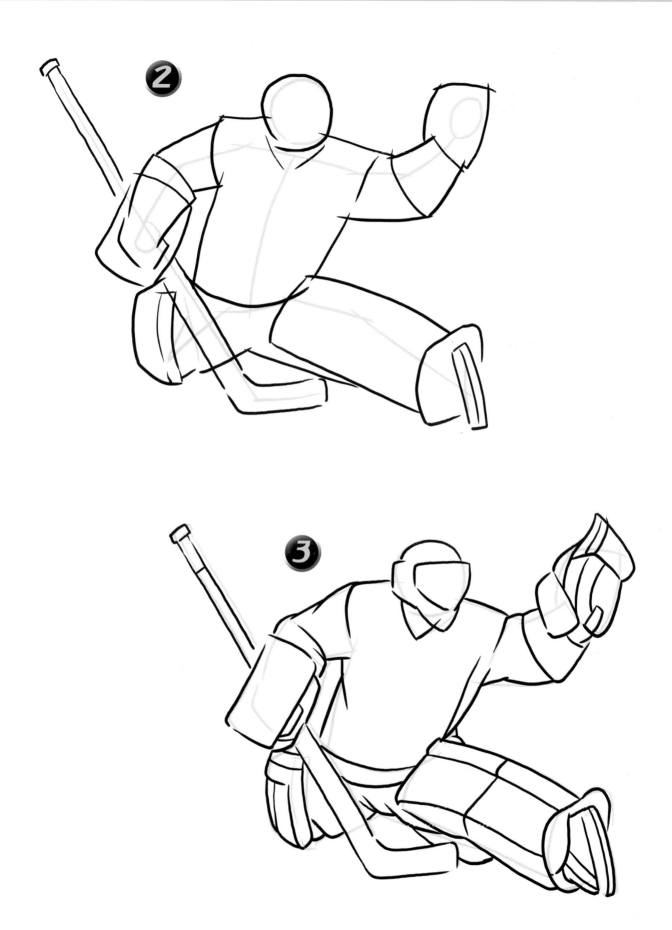

KEEP AWAY

You skate the puck down the ice, but opposing players swarm around you. Will you be able to stop them from snatching it away?

In Front of the Net

While your teammates scramble for the puck by the boards, you wait by the goalie. If they can pass the puck to you, you've got a good chance to put another point on the scoreboard!

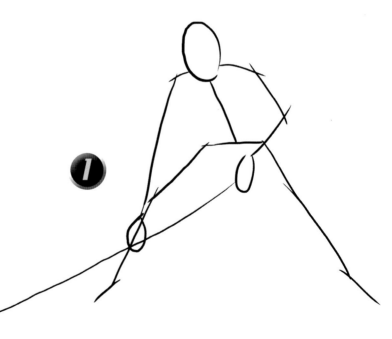

1

CELEBRATING THE SCORE

It's overtime—the next goal wins the game. Your teammate dishes a pass to you by the net, and you slide it behind the goalie and into the net. Victory!

1

READ MORE

Ames, Lee J. *Draw 50 Athletes: The Step-by-Step Way to Draw Wrestlers and Figure Skaters, Baseball and Football Players, and Many More.* 2nd ed. New York: Watson-Guptill, 2012.

Biskup, Agnieszka. *Hockey: How It Works.* Sports Illustrated Kids. Mankato, Minn.: Capstone Press, 2010.

Frederick, Shane. *The Ultimate Collection of Pro Hockey Records.* Sports Illustrated Kids. Mankato, Minn.: Capstone Press, 2013.

INTERNET SITES

FactHound offers a safe, fun way to find Internet sites related to this book. All of the sites on FactHound have been researched by our staff.

Here's all you do:

Visit *www.facthound.com*

Type in this code: 9781476531052

Check out projects, games and lots more at **www.capstonekids.com**

Drawing with Sports Illustrated Kids is published by Capstone Press, 1710 Roe Crest Drive, North Mankato, Minnesota 56003
www.capstonepub.com

Library of Congress Cataloging-in-Publication Data
Cataloging-in-publication information is on file with the Library of Congress.

ISBN 978-1-4765-3105-2 (library binding)

TITLES IN THIS SERIES:

A Baseball Drawing Book

A Basketball Drawing Book

A Hockey Drawing Book

A Football Drawing Book

Editorial Credits
Tracy Davies McCabe, designer; Eric Gohl, media researcher; Eric Manske, production specialist

Photo Credits
Sports Illustrated: Damian Strohmeyer, 15, 19, 55, David E. Klutho, cover, 11, 23, 31, 39, 43, 47, 59, Robert Beck, 7, 27, 35, 51, 63

Printed in the United States of America in North Mankato, Minnesota.
032013   007223CGF13